YOUR LEGAL HANDBOOK

Take Control of Your Legal Action

HOW TO WRITE A POWERFUL MOTION

2nd Edition

A Handbook of How to Be A Self=Represented Civil *Pro Se* Litigant 102
Second of The Legal Guide Series

Understanding the American Jurisprudence in Plain Language
The Necessary Helmet and Armor for Your Battles in Court to Win
the War

~Garrick Chastain ~

Copyright Garrick Chastain ©2020, 2021. 2022

"He who represents himself has a fool for a client"
~ *Abraham Lincoln* ~

No! No! No more!

"He who has an attorney represents him is a fool!
~ *Anonymous Pro Se Litigant* ~

Lawsuits are time consuming. Be prepared, be vigilant, be patient and be calm!
Of course, it is easier said than done. If possible, plan, strategize and anticipate!

This eBook is dedicated to my parents who taught me to always do the right things
and be the best I can be for whatever I do despite social phenomenon.

Here is to you, Mom and Dad, for your unconditional love, trust, and upbringing!

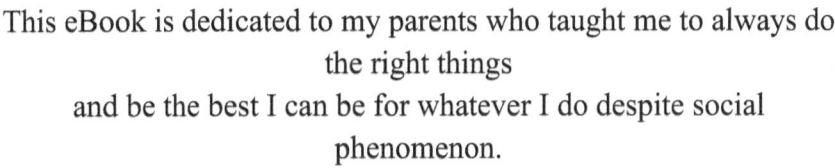

This eBook is also dedicated to those who stand up for justice and the greater good!
Law and justice belong to all and cannot be bought!
Democracy and justice come in hand in hand, one cannot function without the other.

Table of Contents

Leave Emotion Out

Civil legal action is battlefield by "words" put in writing from the very beginning of filing a Summons and Complaint, then, going forward by filing of Motions, Memorandums, and Briefs, etc. When there is a legal controversy, sue or be sued, the involved parties may feel strongly that it is the other party's fault. He/She/It wants justice, wants to tell the judge how wrong the other party is, and believes once the judge hears (or, reads) the "real story" the judge will rule in his/her/its favor for justice to be served. But before any judge will "hear" any party utters his/her/its side of the story, the judge will first "read" the side of the story from the parties, in "writing" on "paper" "filed" to the court. As we are in the digital age, Courts allow self-represented *Pro Se* litigants to electronically filing by setting up an account with the Court.

As the lawsuit goes on:
1. *Both parties are represented by attorneys –*

Every now and then, your attorney sends you court documents for review, which are filed by the opponent making statements that, in your opinion, are fictions. You get emotionally charged, call and tell your attorney how fictitious and wrong the opponent's statement is and ask your attorney to do something. Your attorney, then, reply to the court to dispute the other party's assertions in their documents, then, wait for the judge's ruling. Every month, your attorney sends you a bill with outrageous amount of money for the time your attorney has spent to fight for the justice that you believe so deserved. Fortunately, you are very independently wealthy, and money is not an option so long as you get the justice! However, if you are on budgets with mortgages and other obligations, monthly legal bills become monthly emotionally charged labor of hardship, especially when the budgets are tight.

2. *One party is self-represented, a Pro Se litigant, and the opponent has an attorney –*

Every now and then, you, the *Pro Se* litigant, receive court documents filed by the opponent's attorney making assertions that you believe are frivolous and wrong. While you are reviewing the documents, you are offended by the legal languages from the planet of Mars and get emotionally charged. You feel compelled to dispute the opponent's fictions in front of the judge and starts to write your side of the story and ask the judge for justice, then, await the judge's ruling.

3. *Both parties are Pro Se Litigants –*

Well, both parties may get emotionally charged…or maybe not…Should one party be better prepared with more legal knowledge, better legal writing skills, and additional understanding of the judges' reasonings in the opinions than the opponent, this party might have gotten the better end of the legal pursuit for a better result.

Judges' work is not easy and not simple. Litigants' work is to make judges at ease when reading arguments by telling (persuading) the judges why the rulings should be in their favors based on what legal grounds and how to apply the statutes or the laws or citations from the controlling authorities (case laws) issued by other judges' previous rulings.

Certain amount of emotional expression in your writing, as a *Pro Se* litigant, is not all a bad element to show your sincerity, vigilance, and your understanding of the events of the happenings. Nonetheless, any emotional expression in the argument should not overwhelm the essence of the legal arguments as to the truth of the matters. Any such emotional expression, if ever, should be written in proper tone and professional manner. Any baseless emotional expression in your argument can be detrimental to your case and be construed as without legal ground, therefore, making it difficult for you in furtherance of your legal action.

It is vital to think it through and plan for every document you need to file! In any lawsuit, unless you settle so both parties walk away with something, one party will walk away disappointed; and, often for many cases, both parties will walk away disappointed. Have you ever heard the saying that "Even you win, you lose."?

You cannot anticipate nor control what the opponent(s) will put in writing, but you should anticipate and know what you need to put in your writing.

How The American Judicial System Established

~ *Once Upon A Time* ~

The Courts of America was officially enacted in 1789[i], "**The Judiciary Act of 1789**, officially titled "*An Act to Establish the Judicial Courts of the United States*," was signed into law by President George Washington on September 24, 1789. "

Prior to the enactment of the Judiciary Act, there had been several British settlements established in North America as English colonies, the new nation.[ii] The social, legal and cultural habits of the new nation, however, were primarily descendants of those in Great Britain, brought to America with each succeeding boatload of colonists. Since colonial days, the courts of the United States have taken their own path; changing, developing, and evolving to suit the needs and social conscience of the new nation. The following history of the American jury system, the concepts of due process, common law, and the adversary process further broaden the knowledge and the understanding of the American judicial system. Here, common laws are not statutes but have been, in many situations, originated from England; however, over time, common laws have been derived from American Judicial Courts' decisions and, often time, followed or distinguished or declined the previous Courts' decisions or rulings, the case laws.

~ *The Establishment of The Judicial System* ~

We all learned from our history classes that back in 1787, more than fifty delegates from twelves states went to Philadelphia, Pennsylvania for the 100-day (from late spring to early fall) debate to establish our Constitution, it was the grant "Constitution Convention"[iii]. From this Convention, our Constitution became the rule of law in this land; then, from this Constitution, in 1789, our First United States Congress enact the Judiciary Act of 1789 that set forth our United States Judicial System.[iv] American judicial system is adversarial. This means that the Plaintiff, the person who is suing and making the complaint, has the burden to prove the injury, the wrongdoings, and the loss, etc. with clear and convincing evidence. There are different types of burden of proof:

- Proof beyond a reasonable doubt - criminal cases that are not discussed in this eBook
- Clear and convincing evidence - the highest standard in non-criminal cases that a fact is highly and substantially more likely to be true than false, jury trial
- Preponderance of the evidence - most common in civil lawsuits that more likely than not true, bench trial

~ Focus on Jurisdiction and Substantive Relevance ~

In my previous eBook, *A Handbook of How to Be A Civil Pro Se Litigant 101 First of The Legal Guide Series* (can be found from *Smashwords.com and Amazon.com*,) I detailed our Court System covering Federal Jurisdiction and local state Jurisdictions. A Jurisdiction is a granted authority to make legal decisions and rulings. For instance, in Federal Jurisdiction, there are different Federal Courts in each of the several states, Federal District Court, governing geographical areas within the several states. These Federal District Courts have courts' own "local rules" in addition to the umbrella Federal Rules of Civil Procedures.

It is important to make sure that legal action is filed at the proper court under either Federal or state jurisdiction. If the party is not residing or doing business in the same state as the opponent, depending on the subject matters, legal action may be adjudicated at either Federal or state court in the plaintiff's state or the defendant's state.

When you are involved in a legal action/lawsuit, your case is assigned to a "presiding judge"; meaning that this judge will oversee your case to its conclusion. Judges come from different backgrounds and learnings with different court bench styles in rulings and making decisions. It is highly recommended to read your assigned judge's previous opinions to understand his/her legal analysis and thought process. There are multiple judges in each

Court, therefore, there are many judges in each of the Federal and state jurisdictions. Your case may be assigned to different judges as the case proceeds further. Besides his/her own opinions and rulings, judges will also make references, adopt, apply, analyze and follow other judges' opinions and rulings, if not from statutes; therefore, these opinions and rulings are what we called "common law" in our modern American Jurisprudence. "Common law" is also known as Judge-made law, judicial precedent, case law, or legal authority, which is an important part of writing your motions involving **legal research**.

Legal research is the key to understand judges' legal analysis, rationale, and thought process. We will discuss legal research later in this eBook. **"Reading"** is a large part of your legal pursuit. Knowledge is power. A good reading habit is a must when you decide to represent yourself in court. The more judges' opinions you can read, the more understanding you will soon develop of the laws, either statutory or common law, which eventually will help you strengthen your legal action when writing motions and arguing in court hearings. Often, you may have to read the same opinion a few times, or many times, before you can comprehend the legal grounds. When you receive your opponent's documents, you may also need to read the documents several times before you make a move. Being emotionally charged and putting yourself in reaction mode are easy mistakes that *Pro Se* litigants make time and again. Do not read court documents amid doing tasks. Find quiet time and place, then, read thoroughly.

Focus on your **"STANDING"** (your right in a lawsuit) in the substantive relevance of your case. Identify anything that is not relevant and do not waste time disputing anything irrelevant. *"Red Herring"*, a bluff, is often a way the attorneys use to mislead, distract, and redirect their opponents' and judges' attention away from the real issues. Without legal training and means, *Pro Se* litigants can be easily trapped and misled off the track, especially when emotionally charged at the time of reading your legal documents. Even if you were represented by an attorney, it would be prudent to read every document thoroughly, not once but twice the least, and collaborate with your attorney for your next move. We will discuss *Substantive Relevance* in detail in my upcoming eBook, *How to Make a Claim - A Handbook of How to Be A Civil Pro Se Litigant 103 Third of The Legal Guide Series.*

If you were represented, it would be and should be your attorney's obligation to have you review all the documents before filing to the court. Ask your attorney if you do not understand any part, any word, or any phrase in the document. Of course, any amount of time your attorney spends on your case equates to money as fees for his time. Money spent on and confidence in the attorneys are the two main reasons that folks decide to be self-represented *Pro Se* litigants taking legal matters in their own hands.

Motions

~ *What is A Motion and Types of Motion* ~

We all know that "motion" is a physical change in position. Similarly, in legal sense, A Motion is a procedural act in the legal proceeding that a party, either the plaintiff or the defendant, makes a request to the court to do something. Very much like playing a chess game or baseball game that there are rules allowing each party to make the next step to proceed further. You have options strategically which next step to proceed further. Sometimes, uninvolved third parties may file motions to participate the legal pursuit, such as Motion to Intervene if that third party has interest in the controversy as of right.

During the legal proceeding, there are certain motions have time limitations sequentially. For instance, before the defendant answers/pleas the complaint, if he/she/it does not file a motion to request to revise the complaint based on legal defect and/or insufficiency[v] within certain time frame, he/she/it loses the right to request to revise the complaint unless the plaintiff amends (changes or modifies) the complaint down the road in the proceeding. If the plaintiff needs to amend the complaint, he/she/it must file a motion requesting the court's permission to do so, Motion to Leave to Amend Complaint. Sometimes, during a litigation, the plaintiff may need to amend the complaint multiple times; and, if the defendant files a Counter-Complaint, he/she/it can amend the counter-complaint by filing a motion requesting the court's permission to do so. Of course, the opponent may file objection to the moving party' motion.

A special note that, in most of the jurisdictions, the plaintiff can amend the complaint within the first 30 days from filing the complaint. You should always check the practice rules of the jurisdiction where you intend to file your complaint. Practice rules are statutory, you should be able to access to the types of motion available on internet involving a litigation in any particular jurisdiction.

After you file a motion, your opponent is allowed certain time limitation to reply to your motion in opposition/objection; you, then, have some limited time to respond/reply/rebut your opponent's objection. If your opponent wishes to rebut or to dispute your reply to his/her/its objection/opposition, he/she/it should file a "Motion for Leave to File Surreply". This type of procedural rules is the same in both Federal and state jurisdictions. Each state has her judicial litigant practice rules from the statutes. In some jurisdictions, party may be allowed to "supplement" additional filings to the motion/objection/reply already filed to submit additional relevant materials. Before you initiate a legal action or after receiving a Summons of being sued, it is essential to have access to the rules as reference whether you are represented by an attorney or by yourself.

There are arguable and non-arguable motions, for which we will discuss more later in this eBook. Although all motions are important, certain arguable motions can be makers or breakers. For instance, no party should take Motion to Dismiss and Motion for Summary Judgment (arguable motions) lightly. If judge grants the defendant's motion to dismiss (MTD) or the defendant's motion for summary judgment (MSJ), your case is over. However, you may file a motion for permission to amend your complaint to rephrase your allegation (Motion to Leave to Amend Complaint.), or a motion for reconsideration of judge's ruling to keep your case alive.

Our courts are clogged with cases that if there is a lapse of time (say, 365 days) without procedural movement/action from the plaintiff, the case may be dismissed by the court's discretion for the reason of "lack of diligence". Judges have discretions to rule on motions for as long as 120 days in most of the jurisdictions. For instance, if the defendant files a motion to dismiss and the plaintiff replies in opposition/objection to the motion to dismiss, the defendant must "reclaim" such motion to dismiss if after 120 days the presiding judge or any assigned judge does not conduct a hearing nor rule on the motion.

If your case is dismissed on ground of lack of diligence, some jurisdictions allow you to file a Motion to Reinstate your case trying to bring it back alive, but you must have "good reasons" and "legal grounds", and in good faith, why you let your case lapse in time. Motion to Reinstate is an arguable motion with a high bar and requires a hearing. The Defendant may file motion to object your motion to reinstate. Or the plaintiff can initiate another lawsuit if it is within the statute of limitation. Nonetheless, whatever and however you wish to pursue, always check the rules and the relevant statutes in your jurisdiction and think it through thoroughly.

There are several housekeeping types of motion during your legal pursuit. For instance, you may file a motion asking the court to give you extra time to file your documents. The court normally will grant your request for extension of time if it is your first time asking with particularly good reason and legal ground. You may also ask the court to allow you electronically file your documents instead of hand delivery or mailing in your documents.

Certain motions may be mandatory to get the lawsuit going. For instance, in some jurisdictions, cases involving foreclosures come with mediation program from the very beginning of the case. You may have to file a motion requesting follow-up mediation if you have missed the opportunity; otherwise, you case will proceed without mediation. Of course, in the later time, you may always file a motion requesting a mediation to try to settle your case. Mediation program is always voluntary, private, confidential and disclosure required by law; meaning, what has been discussed and negotiated during the mediation is private and non-disclosure regardless if there is any agreement. However, if in a later day, should one party violate the agreed settlement, the settlement is no longer valid; hence, you case is going back to court for further proceedings. It is your responsibility to inform the court if, for any reason, any unexpected and/or extraordinary circumstances occur after the settlement that the mediated agreement may need modification or no longer enforceable. "Disclosure required by law" means that, during a mediation, the mediator is required by law to disclose any obvious criminal acts carried out by any party.

~ *Why and When to File a Motion* ~

There are phases in a legal proceeding: for instance, the beginning, the ending, and a whole lot of stuff in between. But, mainly, you can categorize it into major three phases while many movements/acts may take place (e.g., filing motions, notices and/or submitting documents as material evidence and/or as references for courts' review) in each phase. Each movement/act is like a battle, big or small, to reach the end goal of winning the legal war; therefore, strategy is vital in any litigation.

Motion is a way to bring substantive and relevant issues, matters, events, etc. to the courts' attention. During the discovery phase, if you know of a non-party, a third party, who is in possession of evidentiary materials, you (either the plaintiff or the defendant) may file a motion to subpoena this third party to turn over whatever materials you believe may be relevant and helpful to your case. Of course, your opponent may file a motion in opposition to object your motion to subpoena. So, now you get the logistics of how the procedure of a motion is about, let us get into the procedural phases.

There are different courts in each jurisdiction at the trial level, such as, civil, criminal, family, juvenile, probate, small, housing, etc. This Handbook is focus on the civil matters. Civil matters cover many subject matters; for instance, small claims and housing matters are part of the civil matters but are adjudicated at separate courts from the regular courts. In other words, small claims and housing (evictions, also called Summary Process (SP)) are not assigned to "regular civil docket" because there is a limitation of the maximum amount of money you can claim as damage, such as $6,000 or $15,000 and so forth, and the proceeding is much simpler only taking a hearing or two to end the case. In year 2020, the State of Florida raised the small claim for damages up to $30,000 maximum in the County Courts. Many judges preside on the small claims and housing matters are junior judges (judges who are recently appointed and confirmed and/or recently elected, etc.) However, regardless small claims or regular dockets, practice rules are the same with minor exceptions. One can also transfer a small claim case or a housing case to a regular docket court for a fee with good causes and legal grounds. Again, please verify these rules for the jurisdiction where your case is filed.

At the municipality level, it has its own administrative procedures for municipal matters, such as application for zoning change, appeal property taxes, open a restaurant, set up a service provider operation, complaint of neighboring nuisance, etc. Each municipality may have its own regulations, ordinance, by-laws, procedures, and so forth so long as these municipality venues are in alignment with the state statutes and Constitution, and US Federal Codes and Constitution. If the petitioners are not satisfied with the outcomes from the municipality's procedures, he/she/it may file a civil action to the regular docket court, either in form of a petition to appeal or a formal complaint against the municipality, seeking justice with good causes and legal grounds. Every legal action must be meritorious.

Phases of Litigation

- *Phase of Merit*

Motions filed in this beginning part of the litigation are mostly arguable in a court hearing in front of a judge challenging the merit of the lawsuit or the court's legal authority to hear the case, i.e., the jurisdiction and standing.

- ○ *Party Plaintiff*

After the plaintiff initiates the legal action, based on the subject matter (type) of complaint and substantive relevance, the plaintiff may right away file a motion for an evidentiary hearing, for instance, a complaint seeking injunctive relief.

After in receipt of the Summons and Complaint, the defendant must file appearance to enter the lawsuit to answer/plea the complaint. If the defendant fails to file appearance, the plaintiff may file a Motion for Default, meaning, the defendant does not contest, therefore, the plaintiff, by default, wins the lawsuit. This may present an unresolved controversy. For certain types of lawsuits, so what if the plaintiff prevails by default when it is difficult for the plaintiff to enforce the default judgment (we will also discuss *Judgment* in my *eBook 103*.)

If a plaintiff has filed multiple lawsuits/complaints against multiple defendants separately at multiple jurisdictions within the state over the same cause of action (the same injury), the plaintiff may file a Motion to Consolidate all the cases to one jurisdiction/location to get all the separate cases into one case for adjudication.

o *Party Defendant*

The defendant must file appearance to enter the lawsuit, then, to answer/plea the complaint. If the defendant fails to file appearance, the plaintiff may file a motion for default, meaning, the defendant does not contest, therefore, the plaintiff, by default, wins the lawsuit.

There are several motions the defendant may file before answering the complaint to challenge the sustainability (or, the standing) of the case. For instance, the defendant may ask the court to request the plaintiff to revise the complaint due to defective or unclear or unintelligible statement or allegation in the complaint; however, this must be done within, normally, 30 days after filing appearance. Motion to Dismiss is the most common first motion filed by the defendants when the Court's jurisdiction to adjudicate the action is challenged. Motion to Strike (the legal sufficiency alleged in the complaint is challenged) and Motion for Summary Judgment (no genuine issue of material facts is challenged) are also common legal tactics in attempt to end the lawsuit. The defendant may also file a Motion for Evidentiary Hearing asking the court to have the plaintiff show cause and show material facts to prove merit; in addition, the defendant may also file Counter-Claim/Complaint at the time when filing answers to the Plaintiff's complaint.

- o *Third Party*

After receiving the Summons and Complaint, the defendant may bring in another party/other parties (enjoin) if he/she/it believes this third party is liable for the plaintiff's claim. A non-involving party may also file a motion asking the court to add him/her/it as a third-party defendant to get involved. This type of act from a third-party usually involves cases with higher degree of complexity.

- *Phase of Discovery*

Although the plaintiff is the master of the lawsuit, it is the plaintiff's burden to prove the merits of the case.

For the plaintiff, he/she/it may serve the defendant(s) interrogatories and request for production immediately after serving the summons and the complaint. Normally the defendant(s) has 60 days to answer questions and requests (check your state statutes and local rules.) With good cause and legal ground, the defendant may ask for extra time to answer. If the defendant does not answer for longer than rules allow and does not ask for extra time, the plaintiff may file a Motion to Compel the defendant to answer. If the defendant persists in failure to answer after motion to compel, the plaintiff may file motion for judgment for damtges.

By the same token, the defendant, after filing appearance, may immediately serve interrogatories and request for production to plaintiff based on the allegation. The defendant may ask the court to compel the plaintiff to answer if the plaintiff does not answer. After the judge's order to answer, the defendant may file Motion for Non-Suit if the plaintiff continue to refuse to answer; thereafter, if judge rules in the defendant's favor, the case is over. At this time, the plaintiff may either immediately file answers asking for reconsideration with good causes and legal grounds. If the plaintiff's answers appear to be bogus with objections to every question, the defendant may file Motion for Non-Suit as well for non-compliance to the rules to end the lawsuit.

Both parties may file subpoenas asking the other party to submit documents relevant to the lawsuit. For self-represented *Pro Se* litigants, subpoenas must be file at court for permission before serving the other party. Subpoenas may be served to a third-party who is not a party in the lawsuit to hand over documents. Before serving subpoenas, make sure to follow the rules as to the process of service of subpoenas.

Immediately after the lawsuit is filed, both parties may serve the other party Letter of Preservation to preserve potential material facts to prevent evidence from being destroyed. If a party receives such letter of preservation, he/she/it must preserve all relevant information including data in paper and electronic forms including business records, phone records, email records, etc., or else be sanctioned for monetary damages to the opponent.

Before trial, any party may conduct depositions for testimony. Depositions normally are based on the findings from the interrogatories and requests for productions. You are face-to-face to the opponent or the witness asking questions directly for the information you need for your case. Deposition is costly. You need a conference room and a court reporter who transcribes all the speaking words from the deposition. The reporter will produce transcripts of the deposition. It is your obligation to provide an original copy of the transcript to your opponent and a sealed original copy to the court. These days, many depositions are conducted virtually through videos from mobile devices assessing to internet, such as computers.

During the depositions, you may ask questions based on certain documents for confirmation and label your documents as exhibits of evidence for trial. During and after the discovery, you should have a list of material facts and witnesses that you want to submit to the court as exhibits of evidence for trial. We will discuss material fact and evidence in another *eBook* in detail.

- *Phase of Trial*

Not all the cases have jury trials. At the time of filing your Summons and Complaint, as a plaintiff, you may file asking for a jury trial. You may not get a jury trial even if you ask for one. Most of the lawsuits have bench trials, meaning tried in front of judges. There is a jury trial fee. This fee may be refunded to you if you do not get the jury trial asked. Very often, defendants file asking for jury trials regardless of whether will get it or not.

Before the trial, the court will set a pre-trial conference and have both parties come to an agreement of the issues and list of exhibits for trial. Very often, the case may be resolved and settled at this pre-trial conference. Before the pre-trial conference, the courts like to ask both parties to settle if possible. Of course, at any time during the legal proceeding, any party may ask for mediation and/or settlement. Sometimes, party will file Motion to Compromise to settle the case, but the opponent has no obligation to reply to such motion.

Many attorneys conduct depositions right before or during the trials strategically. This is even more costly because the transcripts from the depositions must be produced for the next day for the trial, not to mention the extra costs if you want to have the transcript of the trial available to you immediately for the trial next day.

A trial may last for any number of hours or days. For most bench trial cases, it probably only lasts for one or one half of a day and no more than a few days.

~ *A Double-Edged Sword* ~

A motion can be a double-edged sword if not well planned and written.

Here was a case that the plaintiff filed a Claim in a Small Claim court for money owned to his services performed of $4,000.00. The defendant not only transferred the case to a regular docket Civil Court along with filing a Motion to Dismiss, and the defendant also went so far to file a Counterclaim against the plaintiff. After some two years of serious legal battles, the court did not dismiss the plaintiff's Complaint. After a bench trial, the court ruled in the plaintiff's favor with substantial amount of damage resulting from the discovery from the defendant's Counterclaim, $40,000.00 more than the amount the plaintiff original asked for from the Small Claim court. The best part of this case was that the plaintiff was aself-represented *Pro Se* litigant and the defendant was a nationally well-known chain! One could only speculate as to how the big shot national chain tried to bully the *Pro Se* litigant but only to shoot its own foot!!!

Do not underestimate the power of legal research and legal writing. No lawsuit is too small. Yes, *Pro Se* litigants are at a disadvantage point with limited legal tools and resources and, yes, the playing field may be tilted against *Pro Se* litigants, but it is not impossible for *Pro Se* litigant to prevail.

Structure of Writing A Motion
~ *The Basic Story Telling Elements – IRA&C* ~

IRAC are **I**ssues (*controversies/disputes*), **R**easons (*legal grounds/substantive relevance*) and **A**nalysis (*what, when, why, how, where, who...,*) and **C** is Conclusion. These are the main items/points in a legal brief/summary. Under these points, they cover facts, rulings, procedural passages, and current (pending) status, etc., then, the conclusion (rulings/opinions.)

These are the same elements as when attorneys write motions/memorandums/briefs and the same as when judges write opinions for their rulings/opinions. If you have read enough of motions/memorandums/ briefs written by attorneys and opinions written by judges, you will find the various patterns and formats that are remarkably similar one to another written around these elements.

From the old schools, attorneys and judges wrote in very formal manners with legalese, uncommon big words, old fashion English languages, and classic grammatical sentence structures that, as a *Pro Se* litigant, reading their documents is worse than chewing leather shoelaces. These older fashions of legal writing are gradually transformed by simpler and more concise and plain modern English language in our current professionally accepted legal practice.

Motion needs to be written in professional manner with proper and intelligible English language structure. We are not English literature scholars nor are most of the judges and attorneys. Most of the judges do write very well with scholarly presence. Judges have law clerks graduated from top law schools writing for them, too. Although English grammar is important, do not waste too much time worrying about your grammatical perfection. Your motion needs to be clean, clear, concise (the 3 Cs,) and right to the points to make your judge's work at ease.

You may paraphrase but you may not plagiarize documents. You may agree and quote from judges' opinions as citations and references but do not make them your opinions. Judges do not care too much about your opinions. Judges will take considerations and find facts from evidence and will rule by applying the relevant statutes and laws.

~ Content ~

The format of any motion is also important. It is less of a concern at the trial court level. However, if your lawsuit goes to the Appeal Court, your paperwork will be rejected and returned if you do not follow the correct format. The rules of civil procedures provide you the format requirements and it is not a small thing. The Supreme Courts have very strict rules for formats.

Rules of procedures and substantive relevance are the two components of the foundation of a lawsuit. Large law firms often acquire attorneys whose expertise is solely in rules of procedures to ensure the lawsuits are not jeopardized by not following the rules. Rules and substantive relevance work hand in hand because of different subject matters may have different sets of rules. If you are represented by an attorney, and, your attorney makes a mistake by not following the rules and jeopardizes your case, you may have a cause of action against your attorney for legal malpractice and liable for damages. Many *Pro Se* litigants lose their lawsuits on technicalities of rules of procedures. It cannot be emphasized enough to always check the rules. If you make a mistake, file a motion for correction immediately to show "good faith." Attorneys make mistakes all the time and they find ways to correct to save the lawsuit. "Good faith" is always essential.

To the minimum, in a motion, the litigant needs to identify the name of the motion, plaintiff or defendant, legal grounds, good causes, and the result the litigant is requesting.

~ *Memorandum* ~

Many motions require a formal Memorandum of Law in Support of the Motion. Take Motion to Dismiss for example that it is an arguable motion requiring a hearing. First, you file a Motion to Dismiss (MTD), like a cover letter, outlining your legal grounds and good causes; you, then together, file a Memorandum of Law in Support of your Motion to Dismiss. Court may accept the MTD along with the Memorandum filed as one file or two separate documents.

The content of the memorandum, with separate section headings, normally has a brief repetition from the motion (the cover letter, sort of speak), then, factual statement, history of the proceeding, argument, conclusion (***IRAC***.)

The essence of your memorandum is in *A*rgument section. For MTD, Under the ***Argument*** heading, you may sub-categorize the issues you need to bring to the court's attention based on the legal grounds you outlined in your motion. For instance, this court does not have any jurisdiction (do not have the legal authority to adjudicate the lawsuit) to look at your case, or, you are not the only party involved, or, you are under certain immunity protection not to be sued, and so forth. For whatever legal grounds that you have "not to be sued" you need to have the laws as the "foundation" for support, for which, this "foundation" is the part of *A*nalysis requiring legal research. Based on the relevant *A*nalysis of the laws, you *C*onclude that the court should grant the motion you are requesting to dismiss the case.

At the end, always remember to certify that you have served (have sent your motion and memorandum) to the opponents.

~ *Arguable or Non-Arguable* ~

As explained previously, arguable motion requires a hearing for you to argue in front of the judge. You argue based on the motion and memorandum you have written and filed before the hearing. At the time of the hearing, a judge may already have read your documents. During the hearing, a judge may ask you questions based on the arguments you put in your memorandum. No one needs to agree with rationale in your argument. Your Analysis may be argued in a quite different aspect with a different perspective of the law. Before your hearing, you need to prepare yourself as to why you believe your argument is convincing according to the law therefore should prevail. Here, the law can be a statute or a compelling authority of an opinion from a Supreme Court ruling, the judge-made law/case law, or the common law.

Non-arguable motions do not require hearings. However, if a party wish to argue a non-arguable motion in front of a judge, the party may request such motion to be heard in front of a judge at the time of filing by writing such request in the motion. Each court has a timetable indicates when a motion be ruled by sending out notices to the parties.

Motion as Powerful Tool

~ *Legal Grounds and Good Causes* ~

Motions require legal grounds and good causes that are circumstances allowing you to make a move under the rules of civil procedures and laws. In **rules** of civil procedures, for instance, litigants are allowed extra time needed to complete the necessary filing (the **legal grounds**) but they must have good **reasons** (the **good causes**.) Let us examine two common practices, *Motion to Dismiss* and *Motion for Extension of Time*.

For instance, as a defendant, a *Pro Se* litigant, at the time when you need to answer the complaint, you have an emergency for medical treatment. Based on your good causes of needing medical urgent care, the rules would allow you to have extra time to answer the plaintiff's complaint by filing a **Motion for Extension of Time** to answer/plea. This should be an easy motion without much of extensive legal research to back up your cause. However, if you are represented by an attorney, your motion may or may not be granted because your attorney is not in medical urgent care; unless the case involved, for instance, with a third party that your attorney needs your attention to sort out the events, but you are sick. Nonetheless, if your attorney is in medical urgent care, he/she may file the motion for extension of time and be granted. This is not an arguable motion, no hearing required, and the judge will rule on paper. "Rule on paper" means that the judge will read the motion to either grant or deny the motion without a hearing.

Most of the motions for extra time do not extend more than 30 days, sometimes even less based on the good cause and legal ground. If you need an extra of a couple of months, you may have to file a Motion for Continuance to stop the proceeding for a reasonable length of time. Judge may or may not grant your request or may grant you a shorter amount of time depending on your circumstances. Being a *Pro Se* litigant or not, as common as the practice of Motion for Extension of Time, one should not take it lightly without good causes. Even though the rules allow you to take extra time but if you abuse the rules too many times without good causes, your request for extra time may be denied.

Motion to Dismiss is an arguable motion. There will be a hearing for you to argue in front of the judge why the case should or should not be dismissed. A lot of the *Pro Se* plaintiffs get their cases dismissed because of, most commonly, lack of jurisdiction (wrong court or the court is not legally authorized to adjudicate the case,) lack of claim (even though you put allegations in your Complaint but you did not claim what damages you have suffered,) lack of proper process of services (you did not serve the defendant of your Summons and Complaint or the defendant was not served properly,) wrong defendant, wrong plaintiff, frivolous allegations, and so forth.

~ Legal Research ~

In layman's term, legal research is the task to try to understand the laws from various sources. It is the most important task in a lawsuit. The various sources provide how the laws are adopted and enacted, how judges interpret the laws, how attorneys apply the laws, and why these laws are established, and so forth.

When writing an arguable motion, you will need to do legal research to back up your argument. In the hearing for your arguable motion, you need to refer to your legal research collected and written in your argument. As there are many ways leading to Rome, so are many ways leading to do your legal research.

There are commercially run companies selling information for legal research. A lot of law firms subscribe legal information with hefty fees so that their attorneys can do a more thorough job when writing legal documents. Solo law firms may not be able to afford the expensive subscriptions so they will have to go to the Courts' Legal Libraries to do the legal research, where most of the *Pro Se* litigants will go for their legal research. Majority of the state Courts' Legal Libraries subscribe and provide search engines for legal information in addition to all the law books. The Court Librarians may assist you how to find or search. Court librarians should receive basic training as to what those flags and symbols mean from case laws and how to do a search more effectively from those commercial legal engines, but the Librarian will not and cannot give you any legal advice.

There is no better way to start the legal research but to just do it by starting from a point where you feel most researchable depending on the subject matter and the substantive relevance of your case. Search on Internet is what most of the *Pro Se* litigants will start; however, you probably will not get the most of what you need for your legal writing, perhaps about only 10to 20 percent the most. Certainly, the legal information sold by the commercially run companies should provide you most of the legal information if you know how to find it then reference it in your writing. For *Pro Se* litigants, the court legal library where your case filed is the best place for your legal research because not only the library may subscribe legal information search engine, but you may also find the previous opinions issued by the same judge who is presiding on your case. If the court where your case filed is too far of a distance for you, then, any court library closest to you should do.

If you are writing a motion to object your opponent's motion, for *Pro Se* litigant, it is not a bad idea to understand all the citations (the quotations from other lawsuits) in your opponent's motion. Most of these citations are excerpts from judges' opinions from other lawsuits that may or may not be relevant to your case. Not all the citations from your opponent's motion are still good laws or the right citations/case laws relevant to your case. An attorney may or may not do any better legal research task than any of the *Pro Se* litigant. You need to bring to the Judge's attention if the opponent's citations are misleading; otherwise, the judge will take it from face value and consider it a good authority. Again, part of your job is to make your judge's life a little easier to help yourself. Judges will not verify anyone's citation is relevant or not. **It is part of your due diligence to safeguard your legal action.** It is easily shown how much effort you put in from your paperwork.

~ *Arguments* ~

Legal argument in writing is challenging, especially for legally untrained *Pro Se* litigants and judges know it. As previously discussed in "***Structure of Writing a Motion***", no need to add fancy and/or impressive "big" words but be clean, clear, concise, and plain to the points.

Pro Se litigants often ignore a crucial reality that what you think and what you believe are much less relevant to what your judge will consider unless you lay out reasonings based on the statutes or the common laws/case laws from other judges have ruled on similar subject matters.

Always start with a draft of your motion. Your writing should be easy to follow and to reference from sentence to sentence, from paragraph to paragraph, from section to section, and from page to page that make sense. So, start by writing a draft with an outline. For each line item in your outline, write down what are the points. For each point, write down your thought process. After writing down all the thought process for the entire draft, put it aside and take a break. Review and edit your draft, not once, but at least a couple of times. Take another break, then, come back to write your formal Motion for filing.

So, let us examine the following "argument" extracted from a Motion to Dismiss filed in Connecticut Superior Court on legal ground of lack of jurisdiction due to insufficient process of service:

> """Connecticut's Supreme Court recognizes that "[t]he Superior Court may exercise jurisdiction over a person only if that person has been properly served with process, has consented to jurisdiction of the court or has waived any objection to the court's exercise of personal jurisdiction." *Kim v. Magnotta*, 249 Conn. 94, 101-02 (1999). "Although the sheriff's return is prima facie evidence of the facts stated therein, it may be contradicted, and facts may be introduced to show otherwise." *Collins v. Scholz*, 34 Conn. Sup. 501, 502 (1976).""""

Above, the *Pro Se* litigant writes to bring to the judge's attention that: 1. There is a Statute that mandates the process of service., 2. The jurisdiction is relied upon the proper process of service., 3. Evidence is required., and, not least, 4. The proper process of service is relied upon the proof from the evidence. So, the "citation" is the writing of the statute and how other judges/cases have adopted this same statute, here, *"Kim v. Magnotta"* and *"Collins v. Scholz"*. The controlling authority is the verbiage in the quotation ("…"), which is commonly known as "citation". How will you know that these two cases have cited this statute? This is the result from your legal research. The above citations also demonstrate *I*ssue (mandatory of process of service), *R*eason (jurisdiction relying upon *proper* process of service), *A*nalysis (how to apply the statute from these two *citations*) and Conclusion (the evidence shown otherwise) to dismiss.

Not all the points in the draft of motion need extensive legal research or citations for arguments. You will get familiarized with the pattern if you read a few of separate rulings of Motion to Dismiss from your state Supreme Court or Federal District Court.

After you collect all the relevant authorities from your legal research for the points in your draft, you start writing your motion. You will soon find that controlling authorities are quoted and cited from another controlling authorities, where and how the common laws/case laws established. Not all the authorities you have collected can be cited into your motion, more is not necessarily better, but they are your guides for your motions. The "controlling" authorities are the most importation citations. "Controlling" may mean that this ruling/opinion is cited and adopted the most by other judges and attorneys, and it has not been disputed, distinguished, nor overruled by other judges. The Librarian in your Court Law Library may assist you in finding the "controlling" authorities on the subject matter(s) you need to cite in your Memorandum to support your motion.

Your outline, thought process, collections of authorities, draft and notes are your references when you argue in a hearing.

~ *Hearings* ~

To argue in a hearing is a debate to bring your reasonings to the judge for consideration. The party who initiates the Motion speaks first in front of the bench. For instance, if the defendant filed MTD, he/she/its legal counsel would start by submitting to the bench the reasons why the legal action should be dismiss including introducing the citations to support the reasons. The judge might ask common law questions about the circumstances of the case from the authorities were cited, or ask legal questions regarding jurisdiction, etc. Then, the plaintiff would reply with objections as to the reasons why this legal action should not be dismissed based on the statutes and/or the common law authorities cited; and, the judge would probably ask similar questions as to the circumstances from the vsdr laws and so forth.

To prepare for the hearing, you need to thoroughly understand your opponent's argument in his/her/its motion and your own argument, i.e., the reasons why your opponent's argument cannot stand and why your argument should survive. Pay attention, do not get offended, be clear and be calm. Your opponent has the same right to speak up based on his/her/its belief and rationale as much as you. If your opponent is represented by an attorney, this attorney may exercise certain legal tactics that are unfamiliar to you or even to trap you. You have right to ask the opponent and/or the opponent's attorney to articulate and clarify the statement made, and you may ask the judge for explanation of things you do not fully understand. However, judges cannot give you any legal advice. You decide to be your own counsel, therefore, it is your own responsibility for the due diligence of your legal argument.

Hearing can be an intimidating experience, especially for *Pro Se* litigants. Your opponent's attorney may find ways to make you feel apprehended. Do not get emotional, do not challenge the judge with bad manners, do not interrupt (however, you may assert "Objection!" with a very "short" legal ground (10 words or less, if possible, then sit down and listen, otherwise, the judge may get irritated,) pay attention and write notes, get to the point when it is your turn to speak up.

Preparation, preparation, preparations…

~ Consequences ~

Some judges will decide and rule after the argument at the end of the hearing, others will adjourn the hearing and issue decision and ruling days after. You may file a Motion for Articulation if your judge decides and rules right after the argument. If you are the plaintiff and your case is dismissed, you may file for Motion for Reconsideration. You may file for appeal if your Motion for Reconsideration is denied. Or, if you choose not to appeal, case is over. If it is still within the statute of limitation, and, if you so strongly believe that you have been wronged, there is always the option to file a new lawsuit with modified allegation and claims. *The writer here disclaims that the writer is only sharing information and is not providing any legal advice nor intending to give any suggestions as to any reader should or would or could do for his/her/its legal action and consequences.*

In any legal pursuit, there is no winner nor loser. Legal pursuit is costly and is a process to identify the liability, accountability and responsibility under the laws. Under most circumstances, liabilities, accountability and responsibilities are identified by judicial adjudication resulting to a monetary compensation. If you lose a leg during an automobile accident and the opponent cannot give you your leg back, as such, you go to court and ask what it will take for you to maintain a normal life without your leg for the same quality as if you still have your leg but for the accident.

Good Wishes

Should you decide to take on the challenge of a lawsuit representing yourself as a *Pro Se* litigant, planning, planning, planning...research, research, research...go to local law libraries and ask help with questions from the librarians. The court clerks and law librarians may not be able to give you any legal advice, but they can point you in the right direction. Form a network with folks with similar controversies, learn from and help each other of the court experiences. It is not an easy road to representing yourself. You will not get special treatment from any judges, clerks, lawyers. You may even be labeled as a troublemaker, disgruntle loser, ignorant, frivolous and aggressive party who does not know what he/she is doing, and more... You will not get extra attention; YOU ARE ON YOUR OWN.

As time goes on when your case gets more involved and complicated, you may even start to lose friends, no one wants to hear from your venting of your legal status because it is negative energy and unpleasant...BE STRONG IF YOU BELIEVE IN YOURSELF. Few folks will be on your side if you do not prevail...BUT, YOU DID THE RIGHT THING.

To all the self-represented *Pro Se* litigants out there, the real heroes to our American Justice, may your controversies be resolved to the best of your abilities

~ About the Writer ~

Garrick Chastain is an American Advocate for social justice. During a legal dispute, while he was represented by a well-known local attorney, he realized that his attorney was taking him for a ride, charging him a lot of money and did not do the necessary legal work supposed to be performed. It was at that time, again being injured, this time by his attorney whom he trusted, he decided to go to law school and obtained his Juris Doctor degree so that he could represent himself to fight the injustice put upon him.

Garrick is very grateful that he has had the privilege and opportunity to receive a legal education and has worked with many super attorneys and respectful judges. He hopes to bring to the public awareness some of his experience and the necessary basic knowledge of how our legal systems work when facing legal challenges. This is his second *"Legal How To"* **Guide** for those who consider representing themselves as *Pro Se* litigants.

Garrick Chastain is not giving any legal advice in this eBook, and any writing in the eBook cannot in anyway be construed as any legal advice nor any legal representation but purely for information sharing purposes.

Footnotes

---

[i] *https://www.loc.gov/rr/program/bib/ourdocs/history*

[ii] *https://en.wikipedia.org/wiki/British_colonization_of_the_Americas*

[iii] *https://www.constitutionfacts.com/us-constitution-amendments/the-constitutional-convention/*

[iv] *https://en.wikipedia.org/wiki/Judiciary_Act_of_1789*

[v] *For instance, according to the Rules in the Connecticut Practice Book under the Connecticut jurisdiction:*

Request to Revise: "Whenever any party desires to obtain (1) a more complete or particular statement of the allegations of an adverse party's pleading, or (2) the deletion of any unnecessary, repetitious, scandalous, impertinent, immaterial or otherwise improper allegations in an adverse party's pleading, or (3) separation of causes of action which may be united in one complaint when they are improperly combined in one count, or the separation of two or more grounds of defense improperly combined in one defense, or (4) any other appropriate correction in an adverse party's pleading, the party desiring any such amendment in an adverse party's pleading may file a timely request to revise that pleading." Conn. Practice Book § 1035 (2018).

Reasons in Request to Revise: "The request to revise shall set forth, for each requested revision, the portion of the pleading sought to be revised, the requested revision, and the reasons therefor, and, except where the request is served electronically in accordance with Section 10-13, in a format that allows the recipient to insert electronically the objection and reasons therefore, provide sufficient space in which the party to whom the request is directed can insert an objection and reasons therefor." Conn. Practice Book § 10-36 (2018).

www.ingramcontent.com/pod-product-compliance
Lightning Source LLC
Chambersburg PA
CBHW030545220526
45463CB00007B/2990